Develop A Player

How to Play the Position of Hooker
(No.2)

Disclaimer

The information in this book is meant to supplement, not replace, proper rugby union training. Like any sport involving speed, equipment, balance and environmental factors, playing the sport of rugby poses some inherent risks. The authors and publisher advise readers to take full responsibility for their safety and know their limits. Before practicing the skills described in this book, be sure your equipment is well- maintained and do not take risks beyond your level of experience, aptitude, training or comfort level.

Copyright

Purpose

The purpose of this book is to provide the player, family, coach and player's support network with the information needed for positional excellence in the position of **Hooker (No. 2)** in rugby union.

Objectives

The objectives of this book are:

- ☑ To provide the reader with an understanding of the natural physical and mental development of young players in the sport of rugby union.

- ☑ To explain the demands of rugby union and use that information to help guide the player's development.

- ☑ To provide a blueprint for the core conditioning needed to achieve results in the game of rugby union.

- ☑ To provide an insight into what selectors and coaches are looking for at a representative level.

- ☑ To provide FREE access to a professional player development portal **www.developaplayer.com** whereby the player can record and share their rugby development with friends, family, coaches, sponsors and selectors.

Table Of Contents

Chapter 1:
Understanding emotional and physical development

Overview

In this chapter you will gain knowledge of the following:

- ☑ **Background**
- ☑ **How an athlete's brain works**
- ☑ **The role of natural testosterone in sports development**

Background

The brain is an amazing thing. An athlete who wants to be the best they can be in a sport they love is equally as amazing. Both need to be understood, nurtured and allowed to develop over time.

By understanding the brain, the player, coach, and supportive family members can help both the brain and the player achieve truly awesome things.

The brain grows like a tub of sprouts left in the sun. Brain cells get longer and make new connections. The left half of the cortex grows slower than the right in all human babies, but in males, it develops over a longer period, with the female hormone oestrogen promoting faster growth in

1

girls than boys. As the right half of the cortex grows, it tries to make connections with the left half. In boys, the left half of the brain isn't ready to make the connection. After reaching out to the left and being unable to plug in, the right half stays where it is.

As a result, the right half of a boy's brain is richer in internal connections but poorer in cross connections to the other half of the brain. It is therefore clear that regular practice actually helps the brain's connections to connect permanently, so encouragement and teaching affect the shape and power of the brain in later life. So why is this important to know?

How the rugby brain works

Our brains are brilliant and flexible devices that are always learning. Parents normally teach a young boy how to avoid getting into fights and how to solve disputes peacefully, reinforcing that knocking someone over is not tolerated.

Coaches, who aren't aware of the brain's development, ask these same young developing players to forget all those early social rules, so delicately taught, and demand that they go out onto the field of play and be a dynamic and unstoppable rugby sensation.

Some boys are ready for this challenge and take to it like a duck to water, however to other this can be challenging and therefore need a little more time, and a little more nurturing from their parents and coaches before they are ready to compete to the fullest of their ability.

At these early stages of a young man's rugby career we can normally identify four types of rugby players.

- Type 1 – The "Thinker" who eats, breathes and sleeps rugby.
- Type 2 – The "Bulldozer" who loves the physical game.
- Type 3 – The "Star" who is expected to be playing rugby.
- Type 4 – The "Developing" kid who is not yet sure why he is playing rugby.

The role of natural testosterone in sports development

Testosterone in varying degrees affects every boy. It gives a boy growth spurts, makes him want to be active, and makes him competitive.

Testosterone triggers significant changes:

- Around the age of 4 – Initial activity and boyishness

- Around the age of 12 – In rapid growth and disorientation
- Around the age of 14 – Is testing limits and breaking through to early manhood

The boy with testosterone in his bloodstream likes to know who the boss is, but also wants to be treated fairly. Bad environments bring out the worst in him. The boy with lots of testosterone needs strong guidance and a safe, ordered environment to help him develop his rugby ability and leadership is needed to channel his rugby enthusiasm productively.

Boys need to learn empathy and feeling, and be shown tenderness if they are to progress in life's journey. As the rugby player develops he does not need ridicule and blame from his parents or coach. It is important that these role models provide understanding and support. It is our job to honour and steer a young man in a healthy direction if he is to become a well-rounded rugby player for the future.

There is hope for all the four types of rugby players as natural windows of accelerated developmental exist which the player, parent and coach should be mindful of and be ready to take fully advantage of in the pursuit of sporting excellence. Chapter 8 takes a look at these developmental windows in greater detail

Chapter 2:
The four disciplines of great rugby

Overview

In this chapter you will gain knowledge of the following:

- ☑ **Attacking rugby**
- ☑ **Defensive rugby**
- ☑ **Physical conditioning**
- ☑ **Mental conditioning**
- ☑ **The influencers on the four disciplines**

Background

In the modern era of rugby union, there is considerable emphasis put on size, strength, genetic make-up and aggression. This emphasis is detrimental to the young player.

It is true that at the highest level of professional rugby and international competition, size does matter. Gone are the days when front row players had a certain shape, second row players were the tallest on the field and wingers were speedsters with little or nothing in the way of bulk muscle.

That being said, there are exceptions to size. If we look deeper than just the physical appearance we can see the journey these players have been on which led them to become the top players in their current positions.

Rugby union is seen by many as a complicated game of massive collisions, infringements, stoppages and periods of no action. Others see the sport as a strategic movement of players in complex formations achieving superiority in numbers in certain regions of the pitch, which leads to scoring opportunities. Both perspectives can be true, but there are a multitude of additional interpretations in-between.

We need to help young players entering the game of rugby union understand that the game is actually one to be enjoyed. We need to help them understand it is a game of strategy, evasion and the core disciplines of attack and defence, but also of physical and mental conditioning. If the young athletes can understand these aspects and execute them with pace, power, agility and skill, then irrespective of their size, strength or genetic make-up, they can compete at the highest level of rugby union and reap the emotional and social benefits of success.

Attacking rugby

Attacking rugby can be broken down into two scenarios; when you have the ball in your possession and when you don't.

Attacking with the ball in possession

When you have the ball in your possession you have the advantage. Sometimes young players' forget that and start to panic, which leads to mistakes in running, passing and catching.

If you are attacking with the ball, then the opposition needs to react and try to stop you. If you can attack quicker, with greater skill and more purpose, the outcome will be positive.

The ability to attack with confidence stems from three simple building blocks:

- Attack space (knowledge)
- Know you can execute a skill with confidence and precision (practice)
- Keep focused and be in the moment (commitment)

Attacking without the ball in possession

Due to the fluidity of the game, the conditioning, and the number of players on the field, the support role of team members in attack is equally as essential as the primary attacking player himself.

In younger age groups, if a player breaks through a tackle line they tend to run the length of the playing area and score. However, as the size of the playing area and the number of players on the field increases, the defence tends to regroup, meaning that attacking without the ball in possession is equally as important.

The ability to attack without the ball in position, therefore, comes down to three key aspects:

- Anticipating where the likely contact point with the defence will be and be in position to keep the attacking movement going (support)
- Providing options for attacking continuity (understanding)
- Decide what the best role will be in providing those support options for attacking continuity (be a team player)

Defensive rugby

Defensive play has evolved dramatically in recent times, primarily down to the influence of other sports. Defensive structures, defensive roles, and defensive policies have all played a major part in the modern game of rugby union, leading to more strategic thought on how to break down those defensive patterns.

It is important to also understand where attacking sides are most likely to score, and then develop a defensive

8

policy in response, but not at the expense of the natural skills and flair of players being able to defend instinctively.

To understand how and when to defend effectively statistical analysis is very important. If we look at the 2014 statistics information from the southern hemisphere Super 16 sides where tries were scored some interesting insights can be drawn.

Team	From own lineout	From own scrum	From restart receipts	From open play - tap	From kick receipts	From turnovers
Blues	23	13	12	4	28	19
Brumbies	25	6	15	1	34	19
Bulls	23	9	12	2	33	21
Cheetahs	22	5	12	5	34	22
Chiefs	18	12	13	4	29	24
Crusaders	20	10	14	2	36	18
Highlanders	18	11	13	3	33	22
Hurricanes	16	11	14	3	33	23
Lions	25	10	13	3	26	22
Rebels	21	13	13	4	31	19
Reds	24	12	10	3	29	23
Sharks	21	9	13	2	36	20
Stormers	22	11	10	2	33	20
Waratahs	19	13	15	4	27	23
W-Force	22	12	10	3	33	21
Average	**21**	**10**	**13**	**3**	**32**	**21**

From reviewing this kind of data we can start to identify insights on what to defend and why thereby providing a competitive edge over the opposition. For example, if we were to use the above data to develop our defensive policy we could conclude that if a team was to defend well from kick receipts, lineouts and turnovers, then they would have statistically reduced the attacking sides' probability of scoring by 74%.

We can, therefore, look at defence principles associated with set pieces and broken play to become more effective in this part of the game.

Defending set pieces

Set pieces are defined as either lineouts or scrums. Based on the statistics identified above, we would break each down into the elements and put in place defensive practices that would focus on the following:

- **Lineout Defence** – Look to defend the following areas:
  - At the point of catch in the lineout
  - On the short side of the lineout (between the touch line and the 5M line)
  - On the immediate open side of the lineout (between the 15m line and the goal posts)
  - On the far open side (between the goal posts and the opposite touch line)

10

- **Scrum Defence** – Look to defend the following areas:
    - Defend the scrum by not retreating
    - Within 2m of the scrum (both sides)
    - Within 15m of the scrum (both sides

By looking at these specific aspects of set piece play we are identifying defensive channels. By understanding these channels, defensive patterns can be developed and adapted to counter sides that are more likely to attack from set pieces.

Defending broken play

Broken play defence is defined as either defending from when the ball has been kicked to the attacking team, or when the attacking team has maintained possession after a contact situation. By using the playing statistics identified earlier we would again look at defensive policies around the following:

- **Restart Receipts** – Look to defend the following areas:
    - Within 10m of the attacker receiving the ball (to prevent momentum)
    - Behind the first defensive line (in case of a line break)
    - Deep (in case of chips, grubbers and territory advantage)

- **Tap** – Look to defend the following areas:
  - Within 10m of the attacker receiving the ball (to prevent momentum)
  - Within 15m of the tap (to prevent early line breaks)
- **Kick Receipts** – Look to defend the following areas:
  - Within 10m of the attacker receiving the ball (to prevent momentum)
  - Behind the first defensive line (in case of a line break)
  - Deep (in case of chips, grubbers and territory advantage)
- **Turnovers** – Look to defend the following areas:
  - Within 1m of the turnover (to counter pick and go)
  - Within 3m of the turnover (to counter first receiver)
  - Within 5m of the turnover (to counter first receiver running onto the ball at pace)

Physical conditioning

Young rugby union players should find enjoyment in the game and be able to compete, and therefor a certain level of base conditioning is a very important factor that allows them to do so.

A typical length of a rugby field is 100m for the field of play plus the depth of the in-goal areas at both ends of the field, say 10m each - total 120m. The width is typically 70m so the area = 120m x 70m = 8400 sq m. A full size pitch (22m in-goal) would be 144m x 70m = 10080 sq m

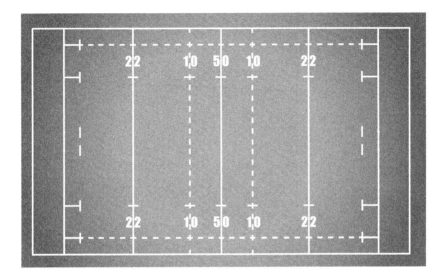

Being able to run is essential. Rugby, after all, rugby is an active game, and to be able to enjoy the game, the young athlete must have a sufficient base level of physical conditioning to be able to compete for the duration of each match.

- **Under 6s'**
    - ○ Field size = 50m x 25m
    - ○ Playing time = 10 minute haves
    - ○ Playing numbers = 7 per side

- **Under 7s'**
  - Field size = 50m x 25m
  - Playing time = 15 minute haves
  - Playing numbers = 7 per side
- **Under 8s' and U9s'**
  - Field size = 70m x 35m (half field)
  - Playing time = 15 minute haves (20 minutes for U9s'
  - Playing numbers = 7 per side (10 per side for U9s')
- **Under 10s' and 11s'**
  - Field size = 120m x 65m
  - Playing time = 20 minute haves
  - Playing numbers = 12 per side
- **Under 12s'**
  - Field size = 120m x 70m
  - Playing time = 25 minute haves
  - Playing numbers = 15 per side
- **Under 13's to Under 19s'**
  - Field size = 120m x 70m
  - Playing time = 35 minute haves
  - Playing numbers = 15 per side

When considering the dynamics and body movements of a rugby player, it is interesting to know that the average distance a forward runs with the ball in hand during a game is between 5 to 10 meters in any one carry and that a back normally runs on average between 10 to 30 meters. That doesn't seem like a lot and, in fact, it isn't when compared to athletics where kids run hundreds, if not thousands of meters in a single athletic race.

Rugby union, however, is unique in that it requires forwards and backs to perform those relatively short distances when the ball is in hand at 100% output, reload, and then go again. Additionally, the sport requires the player to be operating at 60-70% of their maximum in support and then be able to immediately reach that 100% output the moment they have the ball in hand.

By understanding these dynamics, we can put in place the necessary conditioning that will help rugby athletes have the physical stamina necessary to perform in these attack and defence scenarios.

General Physical conditioning

To get an idea of the general physical conditioning levels needed to perform in a particular playing position at a particular age, the Develop A Player organization has mapped out a number of range parameters as a guide aligned to two commonly used tests which are further explained in Chapter 3. Additional, and specific physical conditioning for different playing positions is outlined in Chapter 4, which provides a deeper understanding of the conditioning needed for great rugby.

- Recommended conditioning test 1 - Multi-stage Fitness Test (Bleep Test) for aerobic endurance
- Recommended conditioning test 2 - 30m Sprint Fatigue Power Maintenance Test for speed and power

Mental conditioning

Sports play a huge role in our society, and as such mental conditioning needs to be taken seriously as it can play a huge role in helping athletes achieve success. Participation in childhood sports can be a rewarding experience and a good introduction can lead to a lifetime of enjoyment.

For parents, coaches and support networks, understanding who understand mental development in young players can increase the player's overall involvement and enjoyment of sports. As the adults guiding children in sports, it is important for them to remember that, while there are some fundamental building blocks for success, no two people are completely alike.

Understanding a child's development helps adults avoid unnecessary frustration and inappropriate expectations while simultaneously creating an environment of learning, increased participation, and fun.

Young children (ages 7-10 years) face two major challenges in sports:

- Learning how to get along with friends
- Learning how to interact with authority figures other than their   parents

At this young age, learning to cooperate within a team and compromising for the interests of someone else are major accomplishments. Children at this young stage of a sport are just beginning to develop the ability to see the world from the perspective of others. Parents and coaches should make a clear distinction between what is acceptable behavior and what is not. Since the child is learning, we need to provide them with the opportunity to grow through guided trial and error. It is important to remember that fun, exploration, and developing a love of sports are key elements at this age. If competition and winning become the main themes, these are most likely fostered by adults, which means they should temper their competitive nature in the interests of the child.

Pre-adolescents (ages 10-13 years) face the social challenges of developing best friends and gaining acceptance from peers. Social relationships are one of the developmental milestones that this age group is navigating. They want to be part of a group and often fear being embarrassed. Developing a same-sex best friend is a major task of this social stage. Pre-teens tend to be loyal

17

to their friends and make many decisions based on maintaining their friendships. "Sports hopping" is an example of a decision based on maintaining a friendship. Sports hopping occurs when a pre-teen changes sports or quits participating in sports because of friendships.

During the pre-teen phase of development, practices should be structured that allow for social interactions. Coaches often view social interactions at practices as 'goof off' time. Contrary to many coaches' beliefs, a practice which contains structured social interaction as part of a regular routine helps develop team relationships.

Adolescents (ages 14-18 years) face the developmental challenge of defining who they are and how they fit into the world. Identity development is a complex process that involves applying the training and teaching we have given them, while the teen is trying on different identities. The teen is attempting to discover who they are and clarify their values through exploring different facets of their personality. This process occurs as parents and coaches wring their hands and watch as their own hair turns gray in exasperation!

Often, we see the teen's identity search in the clothes they wear, the music they listen to, and the changes they make in who their peers are. Being tolerant of the adolescent while they try out new ideas is an important behavior for parents and coaches. Tolerance for new behaviors is

18

guided by the rules that the behaviors do not place the teen in danger or interfere with team rules and goals. The second major transition during the teenage phase is recognizing that sports is truly important in life.

The teen makes the transition in identity from 'I play rugby' to 'I am a rugby player.' Participation in sports and being an athlete becomes a significant piece of their identity. Helping the teenage athlete enhance the technical mastery of their chosen sport while supporting their growth as an individual, is a challenge facing both parents and coaches.

Regardless of an athlete's age, there are several common themes that relate to participation in the sport that should be considered;

- To have fun
- For fitness
- Being with friends
- To compete

The social aspect of sports and having fun is appealing to the young athlete. Competition or winning is not the predominant motivator.

Recognizing the young athlete's need for encouragement, socialization, and fun is paramount. If the young athlete develops a love of sports, then with support and a healthy coaching environment, the drive for competition and mastery naturally develops.

No matter the age of your young athlete, there are several simple keys that help sports participation and competition evolve naturally:

- Be supportive.
- Avoid TMTS (Too Much Too Soon); children's natural drive for competition will evolve as they age.
- Structure time to include social interaction and fun.
- Help your teen incorporate athletics as part of their identity by being   positive.

The influencers on the four disciplines

Fathers, mothers & care givers

Sports should be fun for kids. Treat sport as a game, it is not a business for kids.

With all the money in professional sports today, it is hard for parents to understand that it is just good fun to young athletes. The primary goal should be to have fun and enjoy the healthy competition.

Young athletes' compete in sports for many reasons. They enjoy the competition, like the social aspect, engage with being part of a team, and enjoy the challenge of setting goals. Parents and coaches may have a different agenda than your young athlete, and as such they need to recognize that it is their sport, and not that of the parent or coach.

Emphasize a mental focus on the process of execution instead of results or trophies. We live in a society that focuses on results and winning, but winning comes from working the process and enjoying the results. Teach your young athlete to focus on the process of the challenge of playing one shot, one tackle, or one run at a time instead of the number of wins or trophies.

Parents and coaches are role models for young athletes'. As such, you should model composure and poise on the sidelines. When you are at a competition, your young athlete will mimic your behavior as well as other role models. You become a role model in how you react to a close race or the questionable behavior of a competitor or official. Stay calm, composed, and in control during games so your young athlete can mimic those positive behaviors.

What are some of the things parents can do to help their kids enjoy and succeed at sports?

5 Rules for supportive parents and care givers

1. Do what you can to make sure your child is having a positive experience with coaches and teammates. The wrong coach can turn a kid off to a sport.

21

Similarly, conflicts with teammates and peer pressure can make sports quite unpleasant. Help your child work out these interpersonal issues. In some instances, you may need to intervene or intercede on his behalf.

2. Try to determine if your child seems better suited for team sports or for individual sports. Some kids love the camaraderie of team sports. Others enjoy competing on their own. And of course, some kids like both.

3. Be sure to model good sportsmanship, grace, gentleness, and integrity on and off the athletic field. If you behave inappropriately at training and matches, your children are likely to do the same.

4. Lots of kids have difficulty managing busy schedules, which include games, practices, travel, family activities and school work. In many instances, the parents and their kids are spread quite thin and can easily become overwhelmed. Help your child find a balance and make sure they do not have too much on their plates at any one time.

5. Be aware of burn out. If your child has lost some of their enthusiasm and their performance has declined, your youngster may be burnt out. Talk with them to see if they need a break, a new challenge, or a different approach to their sport.

Coaches

Take the time to reflect on why it is you coach. This is beneficial not only for personal growth but also in creating an awareness of changes in our motivation.

- Motivation (why we do what we do) affects our behaviour (what it is we do).

Therefore, changes in our motivation can be reflected in our behaviours and also in our wellbeing.

Research suggests that coaching for intrinsic reasons such as love, joy and passion is associated with better outcomes. These outcomes include the health and wellbeing of the coach, improved coach-athlete relationships, athlete motivation, satisfaction, and performance.

Three psychological needs have been identified as important in fostering greater intrinsic motivation for an activity. To what degree do you feel these needs are satisfied by your coaching work?

- The need for autonomy (the desire to feel that your actions emanate from your own choice)
- The need for competence (the desire to be good at the activity)

- The need for relatedness (the desire to be connected to others)

Those who feel they coach because they want to, are good at it. Coaching allows them to continue relationships within their sport and with their athletes, display more intrinsic motivation for coaching, and coach with a more autonomy-supportive style.

Therefore, being aware of why you coach your sport is an important and reflective practice.

Your coaching motivation plays a crucial role in the facilitation of a healthy coaching environment, both physically and psychologically. Working in an environment that supports your needs will help you get the best out of yourself as well as your athletes.

Sports coaches assist athletes in developing to their full potential. They are responsible for training athletes in a sport by analyzing their performances, instructing in relevant skills, and by providing encouragement. But you are also responsible for the guidance of the athlete in life and in their chosen sport.

Consequently, the roles of the coach will be many and varied, and range from instructor, assessor, friend, mentor, facilitator, chauffeur, demonstrator, adviser, supporter, fact finder, motivator, counselor, organizer, planner, and even the fountain of all knowledge.

In relation to sports, the role of the coach is to create the right conditions for learning and to find ways of motivating the athletes. For athletes who are already highly motivated, the task is to maintain that motivation and generate excitement and enthusiasm.

The coach will need to be able to: assist athletes in preparing training programs, communicate effectively with athletes, assist athletes in developing new skills and use evaluation tests to monitor training progress and predict performance.

The role of the coach can be seen as a very difficult task requiring a very special person, and therefore, they need to be ready to perform in this role.

Chapter 3:
General conditioning for the modern game

Overview

In this chapter you will gain knowledge of the following:

- ☑ **The science behind rugby conditioning**
- ☑ **Conditioning tests and performance ranges**

Background

There are different thoughts on how to undertake the right conditioning for young players and there are loads of online resources that can be used to undertake the conditioning evaluation.

In this chapter the most useful tests relevant to young players has been identified, how to undertake those tests and what the expected performance ranges per age group should be.

Firstly, this book does not recommend any weight training for young players in any rugby position until about 15 years of age, as the muscles, tendons, and bones are still growing and require careful management if the player is to enjoy later years of development and injury-free playing.

The recommended baseline tests are to assess aerobic endurance, power, and speed.

The science behind rugby conditioning

As a child grows, his nervous system becomes more mature. With this maturity, the child becomes more and more capable of performing increasingly complex actions. The rate at which these motor skills emerge is sometimes a worry for parents. Caregivers frequently fret about whether or not their children are developing these skills at a normal rate. As mentioned above, rates may vary somewhat, however, nearly all children begin to exhibit these motor skills at a fairly consistent rate unless some type of disability is present.

There are two types of motor skills:

- **Gross** (or large) motor skills involve the larger muscles including the arms and legs. Actions requiring gross motor skills include walking, running, balance and coordination. When evaluating gross motor skills, the factors that experts look at include strength, muscle tone, movement quality and the range of movement.
- **Fine** (or small) motor skills involve the smaller muscles in the fingers, toes, eyes and other areas. The actions that require fine motor skills tend to be more intricate, such as drawing, writing, grasping objects, throwing, waving and catching.

Physical development in children follows a directional pattern:

- **Large muscles** - develop before small muscles. Muscles in the body's core, legs and arms develop before those in the fingers and hands. Children learn how to perform gross (or large) motor skills such as walking before they learn to perform fine (or small) motor skills such as drawing.
- **The center** - of the body develops before the outer regions. Muscles located at the core of the body become stronger and develop sooner than those in the feet and hands.

Conditional tests and performance ranges

There are many conditioning tests available to coaches and selectors to evaluate a player's current and future suitability in a sport, or indeed, to a particular position either at the representative or elite level.

Some prefer a series of detailed evaluations taking metrics of: speed and quickness, strength and power, agility and flexibility, and some prefer the more simple approach of taking a player's height and weight at a certain age and then using the parents height and weight as an indication of what the young athlete will attain once fully matured. Some of the main tests used are identified below with the recommended two highlighted:

28

Fitness Component	Evaluation Test
Anaerobic Endurance	Running-based Anaerobic Sprint Test
Aerobic Endurance	Multistage Fitness Test or Bleep test - **Recommended**
Agility	Illinois agility run test
Balance	Standing Stork Test Blind
Body Composition	Body Fat Percentage
Coordination	Hand Eye coordination
Fitness General	Wilf Paish Rugby Football Tests
Flexibility	Sit and Reach test
Psychology	Sport Competition Anxiety Test
Reaction Time	Ruler Drop Test
Strength - Core	Core muscle strength and stability test
Strength - Elastic	Standing Long Jump test
Strength - General	Burpee Test
Speed and Power	30 M Sprint Fatigue Power Maintenance Test - **Recommended**
Aerobic Endurance	Yo-Yo (Stage 1) and Yo-Yo (Stage 2)
Aerobic Endurance	300M endurance run

29

Recommended baseline test 1 for Aerobic Endurance

Multistage Fitness Test (Bleep Test) - The Multistage Fitness Test, more commonly known as the Bleep Test has been around for many years and, as such, good data exists to draw comparisons from.

How to run baseline test 1

This test requires the athlete to run 20m in time with a beep from a CD recording. The athlete must place one foot on or beyond the 20m marker at the end of each shuttle.

- When signaled by the CD the athlete runs from cone C to cone B.
- The athlete continues running between the cones as signaled by the CD.
- The assistant keeps a record of each completed lap
- A warning is given when the athlete does not complete a successful out and back shuttle (cone B to C and back to B) in the allocated time, the next time the athlete does not complete a successful shuttle the test is stopped.
- The assistant records the total distance completed.

The below is a table broken down by age and performance level for the bleep test:

Age	Excellent	Above Average	Average	Below Average	Poor
6 - 8	N/a	N/a	N/a	N/a	N/a
8 - 10	N/a	N/a	N/a	N/a	N/a
10 - 12	L8 S9	L7 S1	L6 S6	L6 S1	< L5 S3
12 - 14	L11 S2	L8 S9	L7 S1	L6 S6	< L6 S1
14 - 16	L12 S7	L11 S2	L8 S9	L7 S1	< L6 S6
17 - 20	L12 S12	L11 S6	L9 S2	L7 S6	< L7 S3
21 - 30	L12 S12	L11 S7	L9 S3	L7 S8	< L7 S5
31 - 40	L11 S7	L10 S4	L6 S10	L6 S7	< L6 S4
41 - 50	L10 S4	L9 S4	L6 S9	L5 S9	< L5 S2

Recommended baseline test 2 for Power and Speed

30m Sprint Fatigue Power Maintenance Test requires the athlete to complete 10 x 30m sprints.

How to run baseline test 2

- The athlete warms up for 10 minutes.
- The assistant sets up the course as per the diagram opposite using the cones.
- The assistant gives the command "GO" and starts the stopwatch.
- The athlete sprints from A to B between the cones deviating 5m sideways in the middle of the sprint.
- The assistant stops the stopwatch when the athlete's torso crosses the finish line at B and records the time.
- The athlete jogs slowly back to point A (taking no longer than 30 seconds to do so) following the route

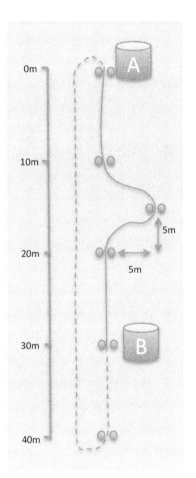

on the diagram.

- The athlete is to complete a total of 10 sprints from A to B and the assistant is to record the times.
- Determine the average speed of the first three trials and divide it by the average speed of the last three trials.

Calculation Example

- 1st Set of 3 = 7.1s, 6.9s, 6.9s;
- 2nd Set of 4 = 7.0s, 7.2s, 7.1s, 7.3s;
- 3rd Set of 3 = 7.3s, 7.4s, 7.5s

The average of the first 3 times (7.1s, 6.9s, 6.9s) = 6.97s and the average of the last 3 times (7.3s, 7.4s, 7.5s) = 7.4s

Power Maintenance = 6.97s / 7.4s = 0.94

The table below is broken down by age and performance level for the Sprint Fatigue Power Maintenance Test:

Age	Excellent	Above Average	Average	Below Average	Poor
6 - 8	N/a	N/a	N/a	N/a	N/a
8 - 10	N/a	N/a	N/a	N/a	N/a
10 - 12	>89%	85-89%	80-84%	75-79%	<75%
12 - 14	>89%	85-89%	80-84%	75-79%	<75%
14 - 16	>89%	85-89%	80-84%	75-79%	<75%

17 - 20	>89%	85-89%	80-84%	75-79%	<75%
21 - 30	>89%	85-89%	80-84%	75-79%	<75%
31 - 40	>89%	85-89%	80-84%	75-79%	<75%
41 - 50	N/a	N/a	N/a	N/a	N/a

Chapter 4:
How to play the position of Hooker (No. 2)

Overview

In this chapter you will gain knowledge of the following:

- ☑ **The Hooker's role at the lineout**
- ☑ **The Hooker's role at the scrum**
- ☑ **The Hooker's role in open play**
- ☑ **The 'dark arts' of playing Hooker**

Background

The role of the Hooker is one of the most demanding on the rugby pitch because of the variety of different skills a player needs to master. A Hooker must co-ordinate the scrum and direct it because it's his responsibility to hook the ball when it's put into the scrum. The Hooker also needs to dictate how the lineout unfolds by throwing the ball in from the sidelines to restart the game. Both roles are crucial to the success of the team because the scrum and the lineout are the primary sources of possession.

Further, the role of the Hooker in the modern game as developed and as such the player needs to perform roles traditionally performed by the loose forwards by competing at the breakdown and supporting back-line attacks.

The Hooker's role at the lineout

Achieving an accurate throw takes constant practice so it becomes a learned muscle movement. Whether the throw is sent in a perfect spiral off both hands or it wobbles a bit from one hand is just a matter of personal preference.

The key aspect is that it hits the mark 99.99999999% of the time. (Because no one is perfect... J) and that means hours upon hours of practicing the right technique.

There is a train of thought that says you need to practice a movement 10,000 times before it becomes an automated physical action of the body. Whereas there is some merit in that argument it must also be stressed that the movement practice must be done right, therefore concentration and commitment to excellence must be the overriding principles

The Hooker has a choice of where to throw the ball in the lineout. Coded calls between the Hooker and the jumpers indicate where the ball will be thrown in and the Hooker must deliver a precise throw every time.

Position in lineout

- **Front throw** - A throw to the front of the lineout must be delivered as the jumper is getting into the air. The ball is primarily won at this position due to superior speed and reaction time.

- **Middle throw** - A throw to the middle is made just as the jumper starts to jump, therefore timing is more essential as there are likely to be opposition jumpers that need to be avoided.

- **Back throw** - A throw to the back is usually made as the back jumper starts to move and thus the ball is in flight before the jumper has started to rise. All three areas of throw require split-second timing so practice is essential.

Due to the size of players in the modern era and the enhanced techniques of jumpers and lifters a Hooker needs to focus on how best to hold the ball, how to build core strength and the power to propel the ball in the air with accuracy and the mental disciplines to retain focus and accuracy.

Because Hookers are not bound into the lineout they also have to be very aware of how the play unfolds once the ball is delivered. They have to be alive to any loose ball that might appear after a deflection and be ready to either pounce on a loose ball or protect the scrum-half if he is gathering the ball. When defending against an opposition lineout a Hooker must mark the opposition Hooker closely and always look to find an unimpeded line to the opposition's ball if it is deflected.

There are numerous combinations of lineout configurations including 2-man, 3-man and 5-man configurations. The purpose of this book is not to delve too deeply into the complexities of them all, including movement, fakes, tricks and awesome moves! The purpose of this book is to give a fundamental understanding of the basic moves and the positioning of the loose-head prop.

There is a train of thought that says you need to practice a movement 10,000 times before it becomes an automated physical action of the body. Whereas there is some merit in that argument it must also be stressed that the movement practice must be done right, therefore concentration and commitment to excellence must be the overriding principles.

The Hooker has a choice of where to throw the ball in the lineout. Coded calls between the Hooker and the jumpers indicate where the ball will be thrown in and the Hooker must deliver a precise throw every time.

Due to the size of players in the modern era and the enhanced techniques of jumpers and lifters a loose-head prop needs to focus on how best to support the jumper, how to build core strength, and the power to propel the jumper in the air with strength and power.

The Hooker's role at the scrum

At scrum time it is the Hooker who leads the scrum into contact. The position of Hooker therefore requires, bravery, and technique. The Hooker binds onto his teammates and the position of the feet is essential if he is to be dominant in this area.

Hookers bind onto their props in a specialised way, they usually bind by putting their arms over the shoulders of their props and under their armpits. The Hooker then and pulls them towards him to ensure they act as a solid unit.

Offside line for players not taking part in Scrum

One foot should rest slightly in front of the other and the Hooker should be on his toes ready to take the contact on the referee's call "engage", like a sprint start, in order to deliver explosive power at the engagement.

In order to be able to hook effectively the Hooker needs to develop an almost telepathic understanding with his scrum-half so that knows where and when the ball will be put in.

The Hooker must strike the ball, usually with the right foot, and propel it through the loose-head prop's legs so that is can arrive at the back of the scrum. The Hooker must also put pressure on his opponent when it's the opposition's put in by driving them or striking for the ball if they think they can reach it first, this is referred to a 'taking one against the head' and it is the ultimate prize for a Hooker at this essential part of the game.

It is vital for the loose-head to work in harmony with the Hooker, putting pressure on the opposition tight-head prop in order to turn the scrum into an attacking weapon and drive the opposition back. Props need to work to direct movement of the scrum, moving side to side to prevent the other team from wheeling (moving the scrum through 90 degrees) and forcing another scrum but with the opposition putting the ball in as per the rules of the game.

The scrum is where the mental strength of a player and a team is most noticeable because the team that dominates the scrum tends to dominate the match. Front row players have a unique role in this area, because they must face their opposite number head-on and win a highly personal battle that requires a unique combination of physical and mental strength. They must be able to work in unison with the rest of the pack so the group can deliver the maximum amount of power, If a member of the pack, and especially a member of the front-row, pushes too early it creates an imbalance and the scrum won't function.

To this end its vital for the Hooker to make sure his weight is ready to move on the referees call to engage. His feet

41

should be perfectly positioned and shouldn't move from this starting position until the scrum advances and even then the feet shouldn't be lifted more than an inch off the ground as it shuffles forward.

Scrum binding

The objective within the scrum is for the front row to beat their opponent into the best position in which to drive their opposite number back.

The Hooker can maximize effectiveness in this area by adopting a starting position that is dominant both physically and mentally.

The moment of engagement is the single most important time for a Hooker to gain the upper hand over the opposition number. Raw strength in both the neck and shoulder areas give a player a natural advantage at the moment of impact, but a player must add excellent technique to that raw power to become an outstanding performer in the position of Hooker and know how to scrummage straight, across, up and down. He must be able to pin his opposite number and also know how to counter being pinned himself and by adopting a perfected bind is the first key in making this happen.

Tight-head binding with Hooker

The Tight-head prop can bind either first or second on the Hooker, though normally he would bind second and usually take a lower bind (meaning his grip is lower on Hooker) than the Loose-head prop to aid the Hooker in the striking of the ball.

Some tight-heads and Hookers prefer a bind onto the shorts because it turns the Hooker's hips into a position and creates a strong bind for the prop. However, it does reduce the flexibility of the Hooker to strike for the ball. Some Hookers prefer to drop their hips when they strike, so this bind would not work so well for them.

Loose-head binding with Hooker

The loose-head prop normally binds first and takes a slightly higher bind, which allows the Hooker to rotate his hips more freely when striking for his own ball. The loose head prop can either pull his right shoulder through so that it is in line with the Hooker or can tuck it in behind the Hooker. Both have their benefits however by keeping it tucked in behind the Hooker allows him to strike more easily

43

A typical set-up for the tight-head with the arm outside the Loose-head. Hips should be touching.

On own ball the Hooker may have right foot forward, on their ball, right foot back but the tight-head should remain with his both feet square and anchored.

Binding against the opposition

- A Loose-head prop must bind on the opposing tight-head prop by placing the left arm inside the right arm of the tight- head and gripping the tight-head prop's jersey on the back or side.
- The loose-head prop must not grip the chest, arm, sleeve or collar of the opposition tight-head prop.
- The loose-head prop must not exert any downward pressure.

Within these binding laws there are two options:

- **Short bind -** The loose-head binds close to the armpit of tight-head. This allows the loose-head to draw his bind in (pulling the tight-head towards him).
- **Long bind** - The loose-head binds towards the shorts of the tight-head. This reduces the ability of tight-head to turn his shoulder in and provides an extra pushing point for the loose-head (this needs the loose-head to have a strong left arm).

44

Body position and the tower of power

There are many ways a Hooker can achieve an effective push against their opposite player. Having good form is the first building blocks needed to achieve that.

- Feet slightly wider than shoulder width.
- Balls of the feet firmly on the ground and leaning forward.
- An angle of 120 degrees between the calf and the leg.
- Hips pivot backwards and chest comes forward.
- Bend at the hips.
- Flat back.
- Head in a neutral position and eyes looking through the eyebrows.
- Clench teeth and push the tongue to the roof of your mouth.
- After the engage ensure the hips have moved forward.

45

The Hooker's role in open play

The primary purpose of having the Hooker on the field is to throw in in the lineout and to 'hook' the ball in the scrum.

The modern game of rugby union has however evolved and as such so has the role of the Hooker. An effective open playing Hooker presents attractively to selectors and scouts.

At the breakdown there are a number of roles that need to be considered:

- **The Jackal** – This is the person who is practiced at regaining the ball in contact by ripping it off the opposition or by being first to gather the ball once it has gone to ground.
- **The Pest** – This is the person who legally prevents the opposition from gaining quick ball from a breakdown.
- **The Disruptor** – This is similar to the pest but is used to disrupt the breakdown once it has become static, this has the effect of making the opposition commit more players to secure the breakdown.

The 'dark arts' of playing Hooker

When the front row is talked about, the subject of "The Dark Arts" is always an exciting conversation. As with any mystical art the essence of the tricks, techniques, strategies, and skullduggery are kept to such quiet conversations in the back of a pub after a tough game, the extra training from the local hooligan on a Sunday morning down the local park or from forming a lifelong bond with a mentor willing to induct you into an order even more exclusive than that of Master Yoda from the Star Wars Saga.

Due to the introduction of ref cams, third match officials and instant replays the "arts" are harder to get away with but there is still time for fun and shenanigans at scum time

In this section we will explore a few of the more well known 'arts'. In essence the loose-head prop would have the following skills:

- He would be an attacking scrummager who dominates his opposition.
- He must be flexible, agile and strong in lineout being able to throw with pin-point accuracy.
- He would need to have good core skills, game understanding and running fitness to contribute efficiently and effectively in rucks, mauls and broken play.

These are fine attributes, however to be an attacking scrummager who dominates the opposition is at the top of the list, and here's a few tricks and tips on how to achieve that:

Stronger grip

- Think high elbow for maximum power; when you drop the elbow then you lose your strength of bind.
- Ratchet bind: the Hooker leans forward before the bind, the props bind on and the Hooker stands up, with the bind now much tighter than before.
- Hooker-ready bind: the Hooker gets into a hooking position, i.e. crouches with striking foot further forward than the planted foot, then the props bind on. This means there is less movement before the engagement and the Hooker is sure of their starting position to strike the ball. More importantly it sets the height the Hooker wishes to be in.

Step1: Pull the shirt over the thumb

Step2: Twist the hand downwards and pull in

Feet and body position

In wet weather it is more important to stay static and solid keeping a strong base with the feet, rather than a dynamic base. A dynamic base is where the toes are felt to be gripping the ground to get the maximum drive forward. For a strong base try planting the feet for more traction. Angle the knees out a little and have the heels of the boot in the ground.

Put your feet back a little further if you are under pressure to avoid being lifted.

Winning the engagement

- Draw in the bind: when the two front rows engage, the props should pull their opposite number onto them with the bind. This prevents disruption and

49

strengthens the props positioning. It gives the prop more dominance and push. Try "drawing the binds" on a scrum machine and see the improvement in push without any leg power.

- If the prop can apply the pressure with his head on exactly the same place on their opposite number every time, then after a while it begins to become very uncomfortable for the opposition.

- Think about dominance, getting the better of an opposite number and making scrummaging an uncomfortable and undesirable experience is paramount.

- Think about pride, even if you are under pressure in every scrum, what is the best outcome you can achieve for the team.

- Remember to concentrate on knees and hips, don't over extend before the snap, and do not completely straighten after the snap.

- Once the feet are set in position the Loose-head prop should not move their feet (unless they need to maintain balance).

Binding

To get the edge over the opposition here is how you adjust your binding:

- Get the left shoulder in front of your loose-head – with the binding over the Loose-head's shoulder the hook is easier, additionally, it invites the Tight head to come further into the engage thus allowing your own loose head to boar in and across putting the opposition Tight-head into a more uncomfortable position.

- Get the right shoulder in line with your tight head – With the binding in line with your tight-head, it allows pressure to be put on the opposition loose head. It also encourages the opposition Hooker to come forward more allowing you to place pressure on the back of his neck thus "pinning" him in an uncomfortable position.

Feet Position

To get the edge over the opposition here is how you adjust your foot position:

- **Maximum shove** – feet square and slightly wider than shoulder-width apart, as the scrum engages, push off both feet and take space. By taking the slightly wider foot position it allows the second rows to put more force onto the Hooker they splintering the opposition pack from the inside out.

- **Hooking** – Right foot forward with 90% of the weight on the left. Once the hook is complete and the ball is won then it is essential to get the right

51

foot back as quick as possible and exert maximum pressure on the opposition plays to prevent being pushed off the ball. As you do this leave your right shoulder on the back of the opposition Hooker.

Cheating

There also many, many, many other ways in which a Hooker can cheat. However, the game of Rugby Union should be played in a positive manner and within the rules of the game (my publisher made me put that in…..!).

- **Slipping the binding** - it is remarkably difficult to work out who is binding on who in the front row when looked at from the referee's point of view. Some unscrupulous props and/or Hookers may slip their inside binding and punch or gouge their opposite number.
- **Boring in** - this is where a prop turns in on the prop or Hooker next to them. Often it is where the loose-head and the Hooker target the opposition tight-head. They will start by making a very small space for the tight-head's head to engage on impact and then drive in. The aim is to destabilize the scrum and thus reduce the effectiveness of the shove.
- **Head on the Hooker's knee** - the opposition Hooker places their head on the other Hooker's striking knee making it difficult to strike the ball.

- **Stamping on toes** - if a front row has some ascendancy on the initial engagement, then they may stamp on the toes of the other players. Hookers are often targets for this type of treatment

Chapter 5:
Additional conditioning for the position of Hooker

Overview

In this chapter you will gain knowledge of the following:

- ☑ **Hooker conditioning for the lineout**
- ☑ **Hooker conditioning for the scrum**
- ☑ **Hooker conditioning for open play**

Background

A Hooker in the modern game must be able to be an attacking scrummager with a clean strike of the ball, have an excellent and consistent throw into the lineout over a variety of distances under pressure. He must be a genuine player with a range of passing/offloading skills and both game understanding and running fitness.

He needs to be a strong driver of the ball with close quarter handling ability and a dynamic ball-carrying option. He must be good over the ball at the tackle and has the ability to act as a second Open-side Flanker and be able to defend the short side and midfield.

Therefore the modern Hooker has to be conditioned in the following areas:

54

Hooker conditioning for the lineout

To be an effective Hooker at the highest level a Hooker needs to be able to throw a ball anywhere between 5m and 15m to a point 20cm square anywhere between 6 and 9 foot off the ground.

Additionally, he needs to be able to beat opposition jumpers with a straight (direct throw) or arched (lobbed throw) trajectory immediately after a high period of aerobic running and physical contact.

The additional conditioning needed by a Hooker in the area of throwing is one of muscle memory and thus the practice regime should be along the following lines. alternating between direct throws and lobbed throws. Each training session should see the Hooker throwing a minimum of 30 throws at various distances with additional practices being done before, after or during each team training.

Each Hooker will find, adapt and develop his own technique. All variations are fine as long as they can achieve the desired outcome of precision, accuracy, and consistency.

However, if you have not yet developed your own particular style or are lacking in one of the critical areas of If you are starting off precision, accuracy and consistency then the following technique could prove useful.

Exercise	Why
Stand with two feet parallel and shoulder width apart	More power can be exerted off two feet than one
Bend the knees slightly and suck in the stomach	Your throwing power comes from your core and your thighs. By adopting this posture to build up kinetic energy like found in a spring
Hold the ball in a steady position above and behind your head	Holding the ball in this position allows your jumpers to see the ball
All throwing movement should be forward	Reduce or avoid any movement where the ball goes backward before going forwards. This reduced the potential for errors to creep into the throw
Follow through and point the fingers at the end of the throw	Simple dynamics. Wherever your hands end up then that is where the ball is headed
Release the ball early to deliver a lobbed throw	Releasing the ball early results in the ball going up first and then down thus getting over obstacle that is in front of it
Release the ball late to deliver a direct	More power can be exerted off two

throw	feet than one

Hooker conditioning for the scrum

The scrum is one of the most essential parts of the game; therefore the Hooker needs to practice the contact battle at maximum power output off one and both legs. This can be done either on a scrummaging machine or in live one-on-one practice but again it is one of muscle memory so that the body understands the intensity that is required.

Immediately prior to the ball being put into the scrum, the Hooker needs to transfer all his weight to one foot, thus allowing him to pick up and hook the ball back. To prepare for this scenario a Hooker should practice weight transference to one leg, squat deeply and then repeat on the other side.

A second area to focus on is the speed of the strike and then getting back on two feet as quickly as possible. This can be achieved by using a scrummaging machine or any other obstacle that can hold the player's weight while he practices, quick strike, and returns. Deep squats and long lunges are also very effective at building leg strength.

Engage	Duration	Intensity	Repetition
Direct Engage (attack)	10 seconds hold	100% output for duration	5 reps
Direct Engage (hold)	15 seconds hold	70% output for 10 seconds then 100%output for 5 seconds	5 reps
Second	15	100% for 5s; 70% for	5 reps

Effort	seconds hold	5s; 100% for 5s	

Hooker conditioning for open play

To be effective in the open the Hooker needs to develop fantastic strength and power as well as being fast and athletic.

In the modern game the Hooker is thought of as a fourth back row player and therefore must be conditioned to the same level as a blind-side flanker, a number 8 or, at the top level, an open-side flanker.

The following weekly work out is therefore suggested

Development	Exercise
Leg Strength	• Knees to chest • Hurdle jumps
Upper Body Strength	• Clap chest push ups • Medicine ball slam downs • Medicine ball throws to the wall

Speed	• **Pyramid sets (four rounds)**
	    • 1x100m, 2x75m, 3x50m, 4x25m
	    • Six by forty (six rounds)
	    • Sprint 40m with a slow walk back in between each rep

Acceleration	• **Twenty fives (four rounds)**
	    • Slow jog for 25m then sprint at maximum output for 25m with a slow jog back in between each rep
	• **Five meter swerve (four rounds)**
	    • Sprint hard for 5m hard cut diagonal for 5m then push hard off other foot to straighten for another 5m

Conditioning	• **Fifty meter sprints (ten rounds)**
	    • Sprint 50m then slow down and walk to other end of the field, turn and go again
	• **The Malcolm Drill (ten rounds)**
	    • Start lying face down on half way line get up back pedal to 10m line go down on chest get up and run through to opposite 10m line go down on chest get up and back pedal to half way line and go down, that is one rep

Chapter 6:
The essential knowledge for developing great rugby

Overview

In this chapter you will gain knowledge of the following:

- ☑ **Young player development**
- ☑ **Catch and pass skills development**
- ☑ **Tackling skills development**
- ☑ **Breakdown skills development**

Young player development

Children go through predictable growth periods known as developmental milestones. These milestones are broken into main areas of development.

- **Cognitive Development** - This is the child's ability to learn and solve problems. For example, this includes a two-month-old baby learning to explore the environment with hands or eyes.
- **Social and Emotional Development** - This is the child's ability to interact with others, including helping themselves and self-control. Examples of this type of development would include a boy knowing how to take turns in games at school.

- **Fine Motor Skill Development** - This is the child's ability to use small muscles, specifically their hands and fingers, to pick up small objects, hold a spoon, turn pages in a book, or use a crayon to draw.
- **Speech and Language Development** - This is the child's ability to both understand and use language. For example, this includes a 12-month-old baby saying his first words and a two-year-old naming parts of his body.

Why is it important to know these things if we are developing rugby players? Well, if we know how a young player develops from ages six into adulthood, we can adjust our speech, words, drills, and attitude to ensuring that players have a positive experience in the sport of rugby union.

Catch and pass skills development

To become competent in the sport of rugby union, a developing player needs to learn how to catch and pass the ball at a proficient level and to work within the team environment. To do this effectively the developing player needs to learn five types of basic passing.

1. **Basic pass** - This is a very versatile pass that can be used in many situations. It allows you to easily control the speed and distance of the pass.

2. **Long clearing pass** - This pass is used most often when you are the Scrum-half or the player acting in that role. You remove the ball from the base of the scrum or a ruck and send it out to the backs. If you position your feet and arms well in relation to the ball, you can pass swiftly, giving the receiver more time and space.

3. **Close support pass** - You use two hands for this pass; gentle and soft to close players. Move your arms to disguise what you are doing, but supply power mainly with your fingers, giving great control over short distances.

4. **Get out of trouble pass** - Useful when a long ground pass is required but you are not in the correct position to make one and are being pressured which prevents you from taking time to get set. A risky pass. Should only be attempted by the highly skilled in dire emergencies.

5. **Over head pass** - You use this pass to get the ball to a supporting player when there is an opposition player directly between you and your support. The lobbing motion allows the ball to travel in an arc above and out of reach of your opponent(s).

Tackling skills development

Tackling is one of the absolute fundamentals of rugby and as such needs to be learned, re-enforced and continuously worked upon during a player's career. If the technique is learned safely and thoroughly at an early age, then that player will always be able to execute the skill and take joy from that part of the game.

Front on tackle (passive)

This tackle is commonly referred to as the sacrifice tackle. If perfected, it will be achieved every time, regardless of the opponent's size, height, and strength.

To successfully execute this technique the following process is followed

- Imagine the target on the bottom of the ball carrier's shorts.
- When tackling, keep the head up and with the chin of the chest.
- Brace the shoulders.
- Make initial contact with shoulders on the ball carrier's thigh.
- Keep the arms around the carrier's legs.

- Keep the head up and to one side of the ball carrier's legs.
- Use momentum to take the ball carrier over the shoulder.
- Twist around and land on top of the tackled player.
- Get up immediately after the tackle and compete for the ball.
- The child's ability to use small muscles, specifically their hands and fingers, to pick up small objects, hold a spoon, turn pages in a book, or use a crayon to draw.

Front on tackle (active)

The objective of this tackle is to drive the ball carrier behind the advantage line. To successfully execute this technique the following process is followed:

- Get the lead foot as close as possible to the ball carrier.
- Keep eyes on the point of contact.
- Keep head to one side.
- Drop hips to lower the centre of gravity.
- Drive shoulder up to the centre of the target either into the stomach or onto the chest.
- Power comes from an explosive drive upwards emanating from the legs and buttocks.
- Wrap the arms around the player.

- If possible pick one leg up.
- Keep driving until the attacking player's balance is broken and you are in control of his body.
- Continue forward landing onto of the attacking player.
- Get up immediately after the tackle and compete for the ball.

Side on tackle

This kind of tackle requires the tackler to anticipate the future point of contact and then track the ball carrier. Once the tackler has positioned the ball carrier into the desired position, then the following process should be followed:

- Get the lead foot as close as possible to the ball carrier.
- Imagine the target on the bottom of the ball carrier's shorts.
- When tackling, keep the head up and with the chin of the chest.
- Brace the shoulders.
- Make initial contact with shoulders on the ball carrier's thigh.
- Keep the arms around the carrier's legs.
- Keep the head up and to one side of the ball carrier's legs.

- Use momentum to take the ball carrier over the shoulder.
- Twist around and land on top of the tackled player.
- Get up immediately after the tackle and compete for the ball.

Rear tackle

This tackle requires the tackler to anticipate the future point of contact and possess an attitude that means he never gives up. A rear tackle is normally used when an attacker has broken the gain line and is heading for the try line. It's not so much about ability, it's about attitude and commitment. Once the tackler has got close enough to the ball carrier, then the following process should be followed:

- Get the lead foot as close as possible to the ball carrier.
- Imagine the target on the bottom of the ball carrier's shorts.
- When tackling keep the head up and with the chin of the chest.
- Brace the shoulders.
- Make initial contact with shoulders on the ball carrier's thigh.
- Keep the arms around the carrier's legs.

- Keep the head up and to one side of the ball carrier's legs.
- Drive with the legs, gripping with arms and hands to bring the ball carrier to the ground.
- Land on top of the tackled player.
- Get up immediately after the tackle and compete for the ball.

Smother tackle

The idea of the smother tackle is to wrap the ball carrier up so that he can neither pass the ball nor release the ball. This kind of tackle should be taught to players who are already proficient in the other forms of tackling rather than use it as the primary tackle technique. To successfully execute this technique the following process is followed:

- Get the lead foot as close as possible to the ball carrier.
- Keep eyes on the point of contact.
- Wrap the arms around the upper part of the ball carrier's body.
- Trap the ball and the player's arms.
- Add your own weight to the ball carrier and bring the player to the ground.
- Land on top of the tackled player.

Breakdown skills development

A breakdown happens when there is a stop in the forward momentum but the ball is still live and in active play. The three scenarios where this happens are as follows:

- **Tackle** - Only the ball carrier can be tackled by an opposing player. A tackle occurs when the ball carrier is held by one or more opponents and is brought to the ground, i.e. has one or both knees on the ground, is sitting on the ground or is on top of another player who is on the ground. To maintain the continuity of the game, the ball carrier must release the ball immediately after the tackle, the tackler must release the ball carrier and both players must roll away from the ball. This allows other players to come in and contest for the ball, thereby starting a new phase of play.

- **Ruck -** A ruck is formed if the ball is on the ground and one or more players from each team are on their feet close around it. Players must not handle the ball in the ruck, and must use their feet to move the ball or drive over it so that it emerges at the team's hindmost foot, at which point it can be picked up.

- **Maul** – When the ball carrier is held, but not brought to the ground, a maul may be formed. For a maul to form there must be at least three players involved, including the ball carrier, an opponent holding the ball carrier, and a team mate of the ball carrier bound to the ball carrier. When a maul has formed, it must keep moving forward towards a goal-line. The players must stay on their feet. Once a maul has been formed, an offside line comes into force for both teams which is parallel to the goal-line and right behind the foot of the hindmost player in the maul.

By understanding the concepts and rules surrounding the breakdown, we can look to coach the skills that are most effective during this critical part of the game.

Chapter 7:
Understanding the body for developing players

Overview

In this chapter you will gain knowledge of the following:

- ☑ **How the body works**
- ☑ **How the body grows**
- ☑ **Common injuries and prevention strategies**

Background

There is a whole science behind how the body works; specifically there is a whole industry that supports the training, recovery and development of rugby players.

A fundamental understanding of the body's energy system, and how it grows after exercise, will greatly assist the player in his understanding, and therefore inform him on selecting supplements to support his development if he wishes.

How the body works

If you are a scientist, or an expert in nutrition, you may understand the difference between Non-oxidative

71

(Anaerobic) and Oxidative (Aerobic) systems, but what do these terms really mean?

Non-oxidative (without oxygen) supplies rely on using stored resources known as adenosine triphosphate (ATP), phosphocreatine (PC), and the production of lactic acid (LA) and do not go into using oxygen to produce more energy. With oxidative (with oxygen), the body uses oxygen to aid in energy production through what is called the Krebs cycle. This whole process is called oxidation phosphorylation. The standard energy of all human motion is the release of energy. Therefore, replenishment of ATP or the removal and/or dissipation of the waste products associated with maintaining our ATP supplies are what happens inside our bodies when we play sports.

A trained rugby player knows how the system works and, as such, knows how to replenish the ATP that is being used. The three major components: ATP/PC, LA and oxidative have the ability to support activities of varying intensities and durations.

All athletes have the ability to produce power and work intensities that exceed their ability to resynthesize ATP. For example, even in a 100m sprint on the track, the athlete slows down due to fatigue. Similarly, in a series of five lineout jumps or explosive scrums, power output drops.

The stages of energy usage in the body

Physiologists have devised a method to look at the energy expenditures of different sports.

The first phase is called the ATP- PC system. ATP (Adenosine Triphosphate) is stored in all cells, particularly muscles. In a sense, it is free energy because the body stores ATP to make it available for immediate use, however, you can only use it once and it needs recovery time to restore. The ATP system is great for short and quick activities because it only lasts for about five seconds and is used in activities like 10-meter sprints.

When ATP is used it breaks down into adenosine diphosphate (ADP). ADP then can combine with phosphocreatine (PC) to make more ATP, but only for a short period of time, around 5-20 seconds. This system requires some recovery time as well. It takes about 25-30 seconds to regain about half of the phosphocreatine stores. These two systems combine for activities like 200m sprints and sports where short intermittent bursts of activity are required, for example, basketball, hockey, and rugby.

The next major phase is called the lactic (LA) system. After the 20 seconds of the ATP-PC system, the body requires another ingredient, muscle glycogen (glucose) to be added to continue.

This system begins when phosphocreatine stores are depleted. Lactic acid (or lactate) comes from the breakdown of the glucose released from the muscles. One of the outcomes of this breakdown is that positive Hydrogen ions are expelled which accumulate in the muscles and causes them to fatigue.

The lactic system is used in a number of sports that do repeat sprinting or high-energy activities, such as rugby, sprint cycling, 100m swim, and 400 meter sprints in athletics.

Training can therefore be designed to help the rugby player improve their tolerance to the buildup of the positive hydrogen ions. Training sessions of intense training, lasting from 25 to 45 seconds, with rest ranging from 20 seconds to three minutes.

The third system is the Oxidative phase. In this phase, as the term indicates, you are using oxygen to fuel the breakdown of carbohydrates first, free fatty acids second and if the exercise continues long enough - protein. Whereas, the previous systems have related to higher intensity work (or power) the aerobic system is more of moderate or low-intensity work, but of longer duration.

The oxidative system should be developed to aid in the lactic system. The development of the aerobic system aids in lactate removal, so that the athlete can tolerate more lactate. Training to develop this system consists of the traditional long runs, but can also have repeats of shorter distances of low intensity with reduced rest (20 x 200m with 30-second rest).

How the body grows

When we talk about training it can be simplified to three stages: stress, recovery, and adaptation. As a player, the challenge is to work the body (stress) through training, take a period of recovery (rest) and then allow the improvement to happen (adaption).

- **Stress** – Getting the body to work
- **Recovery** – Letting the body recover
- **Adaption** – Enabling the body to grow

Through adaptation, the rugby player can gradually develop the capability to handle more training or training with more intensity. As a player, you need to manipulate combinations of training frequency (how often you train), training intensity (how hard you train), and training duration (how long you train).

Another key factor is how the training you are doing relates to your playing standard and position. Physiologists call this Specific Adaptations to Imposed Demands (SAID).

Stress stage

Chapter 3 of this book contains a number of exercises designed to specifically stress the body of a rugby player. Chapter 5 of this book identifies the specific exercise for this specific playing position on the rugby field. Use these exercises and the knowledge of the ATP-CP energy system to design your own specific workout that will help you develop as a rugby player.

Rest stage

Essentially the rest stage should start with warming down of the body using the same exercises prior to the stress stage.

Next comes rehydration. This depends on your sweat rate, but on average, a player will cover between 8 and 12 kilometers a game. To work out how much you need to drink to rehydrate it is best to weigh yourself before and after training. If you lose 1.5 kg in sweat you should replace 1.2-1.5 times that amount. That means slowly consuming between 1.8 to 2.25 liters of fluid at the end of each training session or match.

Adaptation stage

In response to any form of movement, the body undergoes a multitude of adaptations, both acute (sudden, temporary changes in body function caused by physical exertion are termed acute), and chronic (adaptations that enable the body to respond more favourably to subsequent training sessions). The four key adaptions that enable athletes to perform better are the lungs, heart, muscles and, bones.

- **The lungs** - The lungs become more adept at ventilating larger volumes of air during intense physical exertion.
- **The heart** - The main heart adaptation is an increase in size, as it works to accommodate a greater cardiac output from session to session.
- **The muscles** - An aerobically trained muscle has more capillaries and mitochondria leading to a greater capacity to store fuel.
- **The bones** - The skeletal system involves the process of re-modelling (when cells called osteoclasts break down old bone as cells called osteoblasts replace it with new tissue to make it denser and stronger).

Common injuries and prevention strategies

Rugby players wear very little, if any, protective equipment, and their body is exposed to all of those hard hits. Studies have shown that injuries are the most common reason for players to quit playing rugby. Successive injuries over time can lead to long-term effects. Injuries common to rugby include muscle strains, knee sprains, contusions, hip dislocations, and facial injury.

Most Common Rugby Injuries

There are many injuries that can take place during the course of a game, the most common ones are identified below:

- **Muscle Strain** - When competing in rugby or practicing for competition, the muscles are stressed and stretched repeatedly. A hard-driving scrum or a move to evade a defender can place the muscles at risk of tearing. When the muscle tears it becomes weaker, pain and tenderness set in, and some slight swelling and bruising may occur. A minor strain will respond to ice, rest, and allow a return to full activity within one to two weeks.

- **Knee Sprain -** Any of the ligaments in the knee are subject to sprain in a hard-hitting rugby game. The most common sprains include the anterior cruciate ligament (ACL) and the medial collateral ligament (MCL.) The ACL is often torn when the foot and lower leg are planted, but the upper leg rotates. The MCL is commonly sprained by contact from another player on the outside of the knee. The severity of the sprain is determined by the amount of tearing present in the ligament, with the worst being a complete rupture. Minor sprains may take two to

78

three weeks for recovery, while a total tear may take eight weeks. Ice, and immobilization will help with recovery.

- **Bruises and Contusions** - As with any contact sport, bruises and contusions are very common in rugby. Players are being impacted in many directions, and those hard-hits result in blood vessels under the skin rupturing which causes swelling, pain, discoloration, and tenderness. Most contusions can be treated with ice. Deeper contusions in the muscle tissue may require rest and a gradual return to play.

Injury prevention strategies

To compete in the modern game of rugby a rugby player should develop a natural protective layering (musculature) and be strong enough to withstand the physical impacts of the game.

Practicing the game and becoming proficient in the skills of rugby condition the body when delivering a tackle, or taking one, which will help the player avoid some of the most common injuries in rugby.

Use of the minimal protective equipment such as a mouth guard would help shield the body from some of the usual injuries encountered in a game or during practice.

Strength training will help build protective muscle tissue over the bones and joints and will help keep the body healthy for games and speed recovery should an injury occur.

Flexibility is vital to condition the body to cope when it is twisted and contorted at different angles during tackles or when avoiding a defender, so a good flexibility routine is essential.

The top three rugby stretches

Stretching is one of the most under-utilized techniques for improving athletic performance, preventing sports injury, and properly rehabilitating sprain and strain injury. Don't make the mistake of thinking that something as simple as stretching won't be useful. The following three essential stretching exercises are very beneficial for rugby players.

- **Reaching-up shoulder stretch** - Place one hand behind your back and then reach up between your shoulder blades.

- **Lying knee roll-over stretch** - While lying on your back, bend your knees and let them fall to one side. Keep your arms out to the side and let your back and hips rotate with your knees.

- **Kneeling Quad Stretch** - Kneel on one foot and the other knee. If needed, hold on to something to keep your balance and then push your hips forward.

81

Chapter 8:
Natural windows for player development

Overview

In this chapter you will gain knowledge of the following:

- ☑ **Development windows**
- ☑ **Long Term Player Development Pathways (LTDP)**

Background

Developing players, who are committed to their own success, continually look to improve themselves. Whether it be developing their attacking, defensive, physical or mental conditioning, or working on the core essentials of positional specific excellence, they desire to be the very best they can be.

As humans, we are continually learning and developing new skills through life experiences. There are, however, some extraordinary development windows during the younger years of five to seventeen whereby the developing rugby player can accelerate the skills needed for exceptional rugby.

Development windows

Strength and conditioning is an absolutely essential part of developing a competent player in the sport of rugby union.

However, to progress, the player, family, coach and support network must understand the 'windows' of development within the young athlete.

- **Skills window** – This occurs between the approximate ages of 8 to 11 for girls and 9 to 12 years of age for boys.
- **Speed window -** During the growth spurt for boys it is important for coaches to understand the Long Term Player Development Pathway (FTPDP) if they are to successfully take advantage of opportunities for skill and fitness development and maintain the players commitment to the sport they love.

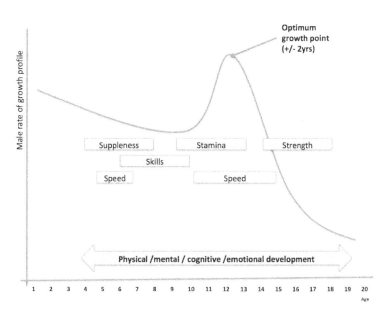

There is ample evidence showing that children and teenagers can improve in strength (Falk and Tenembaum, 1996, Payne et al., 1997), anaerobic fitness (Tolfrey, 2007) and aerobic fitness (Baquet et al., 2003) as well as speed, balance and stability (Gilligan et al., 2005). Further, resistance training, when completed under the qualified supervision of an adult, is safe, and gains can be made by children as young as 8 to 10 years of age (Payne et al., 1997, Falk and Tenembaum, 1996).

Given the possibilities for improved general fitness within developing players, it is important not to assume that scaled-down adult program are appropriate.

The process of growth and development, which occurs throughout the pre-teenage and teenage years, needs to be understood so that appropriate development of a player is managed in a safe, progressive and enjoyable manner.

Long Term Player Development Pathway (LTPDP)

As regards the adult game, we are aware of the importance of ensuring that the player is developed and prepared to play in a periodised and progressive manner. The latter stages of the Long Term Player Development Pathway (LTPDP), including the "Learn to Compete" and "Train to Win" stages, provide guidelines for the strength and conditioning coach at the adult game level.

Active Sport	FUN	Learning to Train	Training to Train	Training to Compete	Training to Win	Active for Life
Ages 0-6	Ages 6-9	Ages 8-11	Ages 11-15	Ages 15-21	Ages 19+	

Functional screening is an effective method of observing movement imbalances within a player during the "Training to Train" and "Training to Compete "windows which, if corrected early, can improve the player's enjoyment within the game and increase the duration they can remain in the "Training to Win" phase.

Chapter 9:
Recognition pathways for developing players

Overview

In this chapter you will gain knowledge of the following:

- ☑ **Player development pathways**
- ☑ **Competency framework**

Player development pathways

There are many ways for a young rugby player to be recognised at an elite level, and official pathways do exist to help identify and develop those players at club and regional levels.

Whereas it is fully understood that different kids develop at different ages, it is beneficial for the young athlete to understand the pathways early so they can get access to the higher levels of coaching needed and to get on the "rugby radar".

Those "rugby radars" can be very subjective, especially at the early stages of development, and that is why the core disciplines of catch and pass, tackling, and breakdown skills need to be continuously developed and honed through those development years.

Australian Rugby Union development pathway

This is the current publicised pathways for developing rugby players in Australia (2017).

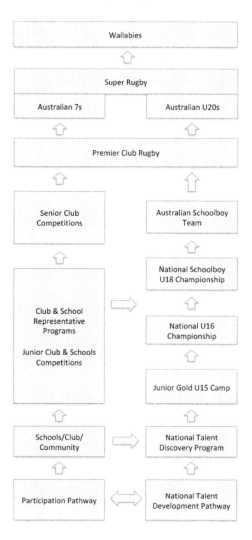

New Zealand 15 aside development pathway

This is the current publicised junior pathways for developing rugby players in New Zealand (2017).

USA Rugby development pathway

This is the current publicised junior pathways for developing rugby players in America (2017).

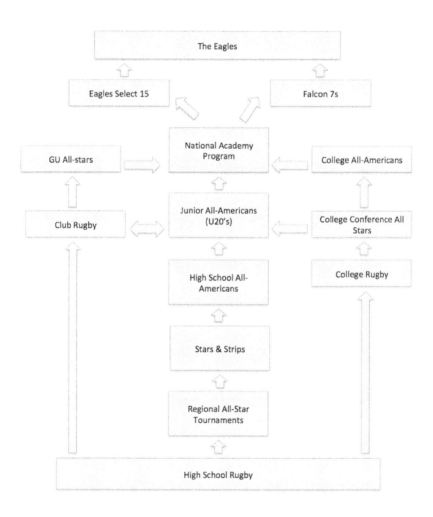

English Rugby Union development pathway

This is the current publicised junior pathways for developing rugby players in England (2017).

Welsh Rugby Union development pathway

This is the current publicised junior pathways for developing rugby players in Wales (2017).

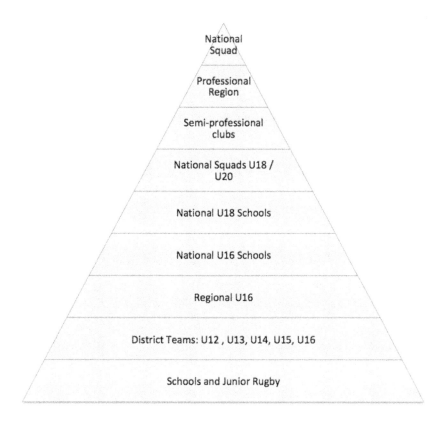

National Squad

Professional Region

Semi-professional clubs

National Squads U18 / U20

National U18 Schools

National U16 Schools

Regional U16

District Teams: U12 , U13, U14, U15, U16

Schools and Junior Rugby

Competency framework

Many players, coaches and supportive family members spend a lot of time and effort trying to identify their development route to becoming a professional rugby player. Some will even go as far as to change region, jobs and even countries in pursuit of development paths that meet their needs. Sometimes getting recognised by the right development officer or national scout is a matter of luck and timing, however that just gets you started.

Develop A Player has developed a free professional player profile at www.developaplayer.com where players can record and promote their rugby successes. Additionally all developing players from ages six through to seniors can get access and record their competency development at each age and against each position thereby allowing them to become the architect of their own development success.

Attacking competency framework

Skill	Description	Level 1	Level 2	Level 3
Scrum	Scrummaging ability in specific position.	Understands role on the pitch in attack.	Performs well at set pieces to disrupt opposition.	Leads set pieces and is effective at disrupting opposition ball.
Lineout	Lineout ability in specific position.	Understands role on the pitch in attack.	Performs well at set pieces and in broken play.	Leads lineouts and is effective at attacking plays.
Restarts	Ability to be effective in restarts.	Understands restart concepts of attack.	Can read restart positioning and adapts.	Mastery in restart situations.
Breakdown	Ability to be effective at the breakdown.	Understands the basics of the breakdown.	Contributes at the breakdown and is effective.	Expert at the breakdown in attack.

93

Open Play	**Ability to attack in open play.**	Understands the basics of attack.	Effective in attack with the ball.	Effective in attack with or without the ball.
Catch and Pass	**Ability to catch and pass the ball.**	Can catch and pass the ball.	Effective in catch and pass.	Effective in all types of catch and pass.
Kicking	**Ability to kick.**	Can kick the ball effectively.	Effective in all aspects of kicking attack.	Mastery in kicking ability in attack.
Shapes and Structures	**Attacking shapes and structures.**	Understands basic shapes and structures.	Understands where to use shapes and structures.	Can adapt shapes and structures to game situations.

94

Field Positioning	Understands Field segmentation.	Understands different parts of the field	Understand parts of the field and what plays to use.	Mastery in field movement and appropriate plays
Rules of the Game	Understanding of the rules.	Understands the basic rules of the game.	Understands the advanced rules of the game.	Has a deep understanding of the rules of the game.

95

Defensive competency framework

Skill	Description	Level 1	Level 2	Level 3
Scrum	Scrummaging ability in specific position.	Understands role when the opposition has the ball.	Understands role when the opposition has the ball and can have an impact	Leads set pieces and has an impact on the opposition
Lineout	Lineout ability in specific position.	Understands role when the opposition has the ball.	Understands role when the opposition has the ball and can have an impact	Leads the lineout and has an impact on the opposition
Restarts	Ability to be effective in restarts.	Understands restart concepts of defence.	Can read restart positioning and adapts.	Mastery in restart situations.

Breakdown	Ability to be effective at the breakdown.	Understands the basics of the breakdown.	Contributes at the breakdown in defence	Expert at the breakdown and can force turn-overs
Open Play	Ability to attack in open play.	Understands the basics of defence in open play.	Effective in open play defence.	Effective in open play defence and has an impact on the oppositions attack capability
Kicking	Ability to kick.	Understands different parts of the field while in defence	Understands defensive policies in defending kicks.	Mastery in field defence and adapts to opposition kicks.
Shapes and Structures	Attacking shapes and structures.	Understands the basic rules of defensive shapes and structures	Understands the defensive shapes and structures and can adapt	Has a deep understanding of defensive shapes and structures and can influence the attacking options.

Field Positioning	**Understands Field segmentation.**	Understands role on the pitch in defence.	Understands and anticipates field positioning in defence	Understands, adapts and has an impact of the attacking ability of a team by defensive field positioning.
Rules of the Game	**Understanding of the rules.**	Understands role on the pitch in defence.	Has a good understanding of all the defensive rules of the game.	Has a deep understanding of the defensive rules of the game

Physical conditioning competency framework

Skill	Description	Level 1	Level 2	Level 3
Scrum	Scrummaging conditioning in specific position.	Has the core conditioning to perform in the role.	Has developed good conditioning to perform well in the role.	Has developed advanced conditioning to perform exceptionally in the role.
Lineout	Lineout conditioning in specific position.	Has the core conditioning to perform in the role.	Has developed good conditioning to perform well in the role.	Has developed advanced conditioning to perform exceptionally in the role.
Breakdown	Conditioning to be effective at the breakdown.	Has the core conditioning to be effective at the breakdown.	Has the core conditioning to impact the breakdown.	Has the core conditioning to significantly impact the breakdown

Open Play	Conditioning for open play.	Has the core conditioning to perform in open play.	Has the conditioning to be effective in open play.	Has developed advanced conditioning for open play rugby.
Catch and Pass	Conditioning for catch and pass.	Has the core conditioning to effectively catch and pass.	Has the conditioning to be effective in catch and pass.	Has developed advanced conditioning for catch and pass skills.

100

Mental conditioning competency framework

Skill	Description	Level 1	Level 2	Level 3
Set piece	Mental conditioning for set piece rugby.	Has the core mental conditioning for set piece rugby.	Has developed good mental conditioning for set piece rugby.	Has developed advanced mental conditioning for set piece rugby.
Catch and Pass	Mental conditioning Catch and Pass.	Has the core mental conditioning to perform catch and pass	Has developed good mental conditioning for advanced catch and pass.	Has developed advanced mental conditioning for excellent catch and pass skills under pressure
Breakdown	Mental conditioning for breakdown.	Has the core mental conditioning to perform at the breakdown.	Has developed good mental conditioning to perform at the breakdown.	Has developed advanced mental conditioning to perform at the breakdown.
Open Play	Mental conditioning for open play.	Has the core mental conditioning to perform in the role.	Has the mental conditioning to be effective in open play.	Has developed advanced mental conditioning for open play.

Courage to Win	Mental conditioning to win.	Understands mental visualization.	Can utilise effective mental imagery.	Mastery at effective mental imagery.

Chapter 10:
Develop A Player developmental portal

Overview

In this chapter you will gain knowledge of the following:

- ☑ **Our purpose**
- ☑ **Free professional player profile for Hooker (No.2)**

Our purpose

Develop A Player was established with a specific purpose, which was to remove the participation barrier for all players wanting to take part in the sport of rugby union.

To set up your FREE Professional Player Profile you just need to go to: **www.developaplayer.com**

Free professional player profile for a Hooker

- **Step 1** – Click on Player Zone Registration to get this screen.
- **Step 2** – Enter a valid e-mail address and create a password.
- **Step 3** – Enter your name, Date of Birth and nationality.
- **Step 4** – Upload a profile picture (.jpeg).
- **Step 5** – Enter your player information.
- **Step 6** – Read and accept the terms and conditions and privacy policy.
- **Step 7** – Click register.

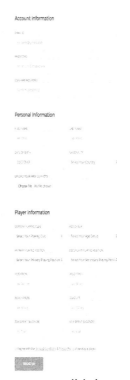

You will receive a one-time password in your e-mail inbox. Enter that code into the confirmation screen and then you're all done.

Welcome to Develop A Player.

References and acknowledgements

Balyi and Way, 2005

Falk and Tenembaum, 1996, Payne et al. 1997

Tolfrey, 2007

Baquet et al. 2003

Gilligan et al. 2005.

Payne et al. 1997, Falk and Tenembaum, 1996.

Develop A Player, 2012

ARU, 2015

www.developaplayer.com

Printed in Great Britain
by Amazon